YOUR KNOWLEDGE HAS VALUE

Bibliographic information published by the German National Library:

The German National Library lists this publication in the National Bibliography; detailed bibliographic data are available on the Internet at http://dnb.dnb.de .

Imprint:

Copyright © 2017 GRIN Verlag
Print and binding: Books on Demand GmbH, Norderstedt Germany
ISBN: 9783346096098

This book at GRIN:

https://www.grin.com/document/512020

Afreen Faiza

An Investigation of Materialism and Life Satisfaction

Correlation Study

GRIN Verlag

GRIN - Your knowledge has value

Since its foundation in 1998, GRIN has specialized in publishing academic texts by students, college teachers and other academics as e-book and printed book. The website www.grin.com is an ideal platform for presenting term papers, final papers, scientific essays, dissertations and specialist books.

Visit us on the internet:

http://www.grin.com/

http://www.facebook.com/grincom

http://www.twitter.com/grin_com

An Investigation of Materialism and Life Satisfaction

Afreen Faiza
Ph.D. Scholar Psychology
Visiting Faculty, Psychology
College of Banking and Finance, Affiliated with University of Karachi, Pakistan

Abstract

The collectivistic culture of Pakistan is perforating with hedonic, modern and lavishing values. People are becoming more concerned with material aspirations and accumulation of wealth. The aim of present study is to investigate the relationship between materialism and life satisfaction among Pakistani individuals. A sample of (N=104) Muslim individuals were recruited through random sampling technique from different areas of Karachi city. Their age ranged from 16-46 years (M= 1.60, S.D=.854). The individuals were administered Richins Material values scale (2004) and Diener et al. the Satisfaction with Life Scale (1985). A significant positive relationship was obtained between materialism and life satisfaction (r=.273, p< .01). The future implementation of strategies for promotion of wellbeing of Pakistani individuals is discussed in the light of findings of present study.

Keywords: Materialism, Life Satisfaction, Muslim, Karachi, Pakistan

Recieved 2 August 2017/Accepted 23 November 2017

Introduction

Pakistani society is facing anomalous transitions during past few decades. Pakistani nationals are becoming more conscious about material pursuits, brand images and adopting other luring lifestyles. The collective values of Pakistani culture are now gradually diffusing the western values because of the advent of modernism through media and other exogenous factors. The gradual upsurge of materialistic orientation influences the psychological conditions of Pakistanis. The area of materialism has been a focus of attention for social psychologists, demographers, political scientists, and consumer researchers (Burroughs & Rindfleisch 2002; Kilboume, Grunhagen & Foley 2005).

1

Different scholars attempted to accentuate the concept of materialism "a set of centrally held beliefs about the importance of possession in one's life" (p. 308) and "a value that guides people's choices and conduct in a variety of situations, including, but not limited to, consumption arenas" (Richins & Dawson, 1992, p. 307). Whereas Belk (1984) highlighted materialism as "the importance a consumer attaches to worldly possessions" (p. 291). Sirgy (1998) expanded the idea of materialism as "a condition in which the material life domain is considered to be highly salient relative to other life domains" (p. 243). While Tatzel (2003) expounded the idea of materialism as "a preoccupation with acquisition" (p. 413).

Csikszentmihaly (2005) broaden the idea of materialism as the tendency of individuals to focus their psychic energies towards material pursuits. It encompasses instrumental materialism a situation in which people shows motivation for material possessions for the sake of self-enhancement and fulfillment of interpersonal relationships and terminal materialism in which there is a pathological and out of control desire towards material gains. It can be speculated that materialistic aspirations influence upon the psychological condition of individuals.

Review of prior findings suggested that materialism is linked with the psychological wellbeing of individuals. Wong and colleagues in 2011, found that materialistic values serve as a way for the fulfillment of needs which includes self-efficacy, self-existence, meaningful existence, sense of belongingness and distinctiveness. Belk (1988) contended that people use material possessives for management of self-identities and personal sense of worth. Similarly, Brouskeli & Loumakou, (2014) viewed materialism as a stress reducer. In most of the studies, the influence of materialism on the wellbeing of individuals has been investigated regarding life satisfaction. Life satisfaction operationally defined as an evaluation of general satisfaction with life by individuals which includes cognitive facets of subjective well-being (Diener, Oishi, & Lucas, 2003).

A literature search found that that there is an over representation of studies which showed a negative relationship between materialism and psychological well-being or life satisfaction (Belk, 1985; Kasser & Ahuvia, 2002; Sheldon & Krieger, 2014). A cross-cultural study carried out by

Baker and colleagues in 2013 declared inverse linkages between materialism, life satisfaction and well-being among residents of United States, Europe, and Asia. Likewise, study carried out by Ryan and Dziurawiec in 2001, found that high materialistic Australian adults were less satisfied with their overall and specific domains of life as compared to lower materialistic individuals.

Contrastingly, there exist some findings which eluded positive trend for the two variables; studies declared that materialism casts desirable influences upon psychological conditions of individuals. Findings mirrored that materialism is positively linked with the well-being of individuals (Dawson & Bamossy 1991; Ger & Belk 1996; Hudders & Pandelaere 2011). Also, studies demonstrated that materialistic possessions increase the life satisfaction of individuals (Miller & Thomas 2009; Polak & McCullough 2006). The inconclusive findings for the two variables carried out in different countries showed that "the relationship between materialism and well-being is complex and enigmatic"(Burroughs & Rindfleisch ,2002;p. 349).

The contradictory linkages between the materialism and its impact on the well being regarding life satisfaction could be accounted for cross-cultural differences. The existing disparity for two variables led us to investigate the relationship between materialism and life satisfaction among Pakistani adults. In Pakistan Majority of nationals is Muslims (i.e., believers of Islam).Here, societal changes can be witnessed in almost all areas which encompass political, economic and social conditions of individuals. The advent of political and social liberalism causes individuals to adapt the new mode of lifestyles.

The collectivistic culture of Pakistan is perforating with hedonic, modern and lavishing values. People are becoming more concerned with material aspirations and accumulation of wealth. On one side in today's permissive culture individuals are becoming more self-reliant and take an active participation to control their lives while on another side, we became more obsessed and anxious to gain and sustain wealth and such practices are fostering materialistic society which impact upon the psychological states of individuals. About the issues above, the primary concern of present study are to speculate the plausible association between materialism and life satisfaction among Pakistani adults.

It was hypothesized that

"There would be a significant relationship between Materialism and Life satisfaction among Pakistani adults."

Method

Participants

104 individuals (48 males & 56 females) were recruited from different areas of Karachi city. Their age ranged from 16 to 46 years and above (M= 1.60, S.D=.854).They belonged to different socio economic status from lower class (6.7%) middle class (37.5%) to upper class(55.8%). All participants were Muslims (i.e., believers of Islam as their religion). (10.6%) Participants rated themselves as having a lower religious interest; (53.8%) moderate religious interest and (35.6%) showed higher religious interest. For preferences of television programs, (31.7%) individuals showed preferences for a news program and (61.5%) exhibited preferences for entertainment programs. They all were recruited through random sampling technique from different areas of Karachi city. The participation in this study was completely voluntarily.

Materials

Consent Form

It contained the brief purpose of the study. It was also mentioned that the participation was on a voluntary basis and all the information would be solely utilized for research purpose.

Demographic Information Sheet

A self-developed personal information sheet was made by researchers. It contained personal information of respondents. Separate columns with empty spaces were present to place a checkmark against each option.

Materialism Values Scale

Materialism was measured by material values scale developed by Richins (2004). This scale is a short scale which derived from original 18 item scale (Richins & Dawson, 1992). It accesses the materialism as the degree to which person sees an acquisition of material objects as central to one's life values. It is 9 item scale which taps idea of materialism from three dimensions which include Acquisition Centrality, Acquisition as the Pursuit of Happiness, and Possession-defined Success (Richins & Dawson, 1992). For present 9 item scale, the five-point Likert scale was utilized for the recording of responses (1 = strongly disagree, 5 = strongly agree). The higher scores of individuals showed a greater degree of materialism. The scale showed sound psychometric properties investigated by reliability tests and confirmatory factor analysis (Richins, 2004).The cross-cultural validity studies for German, American and Canadian samples showed the present nine item version of materialism scale as a valuable tool Kilbourne et al. (2005).The measures demonstrated the good value of Cronbach alpha= 0.82 (Richins, 2004).

In this study, the nine-item English version of Material value scale (Richins, 2004) was translated into the Urdu language through back to back translation process. The main purpose of Back to back translation was assurance for content adequacy. The statements in the final translated version of the scale were reviewed and modified by bilingual experts of both languages. The number of the items, response categories, and directions of scoring was kept same as in original scale.

Satisfaction with Life Scale

Satisfaction with a life measured by five-item scale developed by Diener (1985). It measures the general life satisfaction of individuals. Seven points Likert scale was used to record the responses which ranged from (7= strongly agree; 1= strongly disagree). The higher scores of respondents showed a greater level of satisfaction with life. The scale demonstrated good psychometric properties and found to be a valid and reliable tool. It showed acceptable values for test-retest reliability, internal consistency, construct, concurrent, and discriminant validities for a single factor of life satisfaction (Pavot & Diener, 1993; Pavot & Diener, 2008). The coefficient alpha was found to be 0.87 (Diener, 1985). A translated version of scale in the Urdu language was utilized in this study (Anila & Ismail, 2005).

Procedure

All participants of this study were individually approached for data collection. They were selected from different areas of Karachi city. Participants were recruited from different educational institutes, workplaces, homes and personal referrals. They were fully described the purpose of the study and handed over forms if they showed willingness, they were told that participation in this study was on a voluntary basis for which they would not receive any monetary benefits, and they deserved full right to leave the study. All participants were warmly thanked for their participation by the researcher. All data was simultaneously scored and entered for analysis in Statistical Package for Social Sciences (SPSS) version 22.

Results

Table 1
Demographic Profile of Participants (N=104)

Demographics		Frequency	Percentage (%)
Gender	Male	48	46.2
	Female	56	53.8
Age	16-25 years	63	60.6
	26-35 years	24	23.1
	36-45years	13	12.5
	46 and above years	4	3.8
Religious inclination	Low	11	10.6
	Moderate	56	53.78
	High	37	35.6
Educational Level	Illiterate	18	3.8
	Matriculation	23	22.1
	Intermediate	27	26.0
	Graduate	38	36.5
	Masters and above	12	11.5
Employment Status	Jobless	18	17.3
	Student	57	54.8
	Govt &Private job	21	20.2
	House wife	8	7.7
Preferences for	News Programs	33	28.8
Television Programs	Entertainment Programs	71	68.26

Table 1 shows frequency and percentage counts of the demographic data of participants recruited for present study. Table 1 shows descriptive statistics of 104 participants, female participants were of greater proportion in present sample (53.8%). 60.6% (n=63) individuals belongs to younger age group 16-26years. Around 53.78% (n=56) participants reported to possess moderate religious inclinations. About 36.5%(n=38) participants reported to achieve graduation level of education ;26% (n=27)achieved intermediate;3.8%(n=18) were illiterates ;22.1%(n=23) achieved matriculation and 11.5%(n=12) reported to acquire masters and above level of educational qualification. In present sample 54.8%(n=57) individuals were students ;17.3%(n=18) were jobless ;20.2%(n=21) were government and private jobs ; 7.7% (n=8)of participants were housewives. Majority of participants 68.26% (n=71) reported to possess preference for entertainment programs; 28.8 %(n=33) individuals showed preference for news programs.

Table 2
Pearson Product-Moment Correlations between Material values and life satisfaction (N=104)

Measures	M	SD	Correlation value
MVS	34.12	12.44	
			.273**
SWLS	22.50	7.97	

Note. MVS= Material values Scale; SWLS= Satisfaction with Life scale
Correlation is significant at the0.01 level (2-tailed), *p*<.01**

Table 2 describes mean and standard deviations of variables it also shows a significant positive relationship between the scores of materialism and life satisfaction. Table 2 describes mean and standard deviation value of MVS measure (M=34.12; SD =12.44) and mean and standard deviation value of SWLS measure (M=22.50 ; SD =7.97) . The correlation between materialistic values and life satisfaction was found to be positive and significant (102) =.273, p<.01.

Discussion

The primary intent of the present study was to speculate the linkage between materialism and life satisfaction. The results declared positive associations for two variables in our Pakistani cultural setup. This is in lines with prior findings which suggested that materialistic possessions increase the life satisfaction of individuals (Miller & Thomas 2009; Polak & McCullough 2006) and materialism is positively linked with the well-being of individuals(Dawson & Bamossy 1991; Ger & Belk 1996; Hudders & Pandelaere 2011).

It is observed that in Pakistan during last few decades there is an upsurge of a large number of private mushroom channels which gained authority to forecast the programs based on viewer's choice and there is wide permissiveness to show a variety of content. Modern and lavishing lifestyles depicted in TV commercials, dramas and another source of information are one the probable factor which increased the materialistic appetite of individuals. Also, a rather new trend is witnessed during past few years in which private channels are inclined to forecast game shows which attract a large number of general public. They actively participate in mindless games for the exchange of luxury goods which range from mobile phones, branded dresses, motorbikes to luxury cars. That may be one of the reasons for increasing materialistic trend in our society which consequently perceived as a common denominator for the life satisfaction of individuals.

Another explanation for the present findings of our study is that Pakistan is an underdeveloped country, resources are unequally managed; here economic scarcity, unemployment and other social and political insecurities are more pronounced. In such scenario, people are susceptible to accept and adapt lavishing lifestyles and easily attracted and imitate material aspirations depicted in different advertisements and another source of information. They possibly perceive that possessions may provide a buffer from all sorts of calamities and this aids towards the enhancement of their psychological wellness. This was also proven the fact that the people who possess lack of autonomy and face insecurities exhibit longing for security and control via exogenous factors which encompasses popularity, image and financial and material pursuits

(Kasser, Ryan, Zax, & Sameroff, 1995; Ryan & Deci, 2000). Similarly, the scarcity hypothesis of Inglehart (2000) explained that the preference of materialistic aspirations of individuals depends upon their socioeconomic conditions. It is the perceived deprivations that make people value the goods which were once in limited supply.

Present finding for a positive association between materialism and satisfaction with life provide an insight that people in our culture people seek consolation in materialist goods and this likely to contribute to overall life satisfaction. It is an obvious fact that we all need social validation and material goods provide sense of identification, personal control which contributes towards the enhancement of psychological wellness. Materialists individuals possess a strong urge towards luxurious consumer things because they perceive that costly goods are a way via they can exhibit social position and earn social recognition (Rindfleisch et al., 2009). Tuan (1980) beautifully expressed this fact as "Our fragile sense of self-needs support and this we get by having and possessing things because, to a large degree, we are what we have" (p.474).

It is acceptable to strive for material aspirations because to some extent possessions provides a buffer to different real life catastrophes and energizes individuals to cope with stressors however an alarming situation arise when the materialistic values move beyond critical level in which person invest all his/ her psychic energies to accumulate material goods. This could give birth to a satiable appetite to aspire for materialistic possessions which presumably give rise to several psychological maladies. Prior findings suggested a negative linkage for materialism with positive domains of well being which encompasses life satisfaction, positive emotion, and self-actualization while positive linkages with negative aspects of well being which included social anxiety and negative emotions of individuals (Christopher et al., 2004, 2007; Kashdan and Breen, 2007; Kasser and Ryan, 1996).

Another explanation for the positive relationship between materialism and life satisfaction is that our present sample included 60% of participants which aged between 16 to 25 years; the majority of participants recruited were students 54.8%. The younger individuals can easily become motivated by material aspirations because of peer pressures from friends in educational institutes and other places. They lack resistance to associate themselves with lavishing lifestyle endorsed by public figures and celebrities depicted in advertisements and other TV programs and perceives that materialistic aspirations are way to achieve domination, power and are a necessary factor to lead a satisfactory life.

In the present study, the majority of participants showed a preference for entertainment programs 68.2%. This may foster the possibility of an affirmative linkage between two variables. Prior studies declared the fact that advertisements tend to convince viewers in such a way that they believe that possessions are a way to obtain personal worth (Goldberg et al., 2003; Roberts, 1998). Likewise, researches carried out by Churchill and Moschis in 1979 and Pollay in 1986 found that TV viewing and advertising strengthen materialistic ideals among young individuals

Interestingly, moderate level of self-rated religious inclinations 53.78% may be one of the contributing factors for positive linkages between materialism and life satisfaction. This points the notion that mediocre religious interest provides room for to people to attract towards materialistic aspirations may serve as a way to seek peace, integration and holistic satisfaction. Pakistan is an Islamic republic state due to the assimilation of western cultures the religious teachings came in direct conflict which stresses upon possessiveness, hedonism, consumption, and investments where as the true essence of Islam is not in favor of material accumulation or excessive consumption. It stresses people to adopt a modest life style, and they are answerable to their all deeds on the Day of Judgment (Qa'yamat). The present world is not a hedonic place to get immersed in pleasures rather Islam focuses upon the strong reliance of Muslims on the power of Allah (S.W.T) and Quran for the attainment of harmony and happiness in their lives.

It is also a notable fact that in the present study the weaker value of correlation between two variables provides an insight that among Pakistani adults aspirations for materialistic values and satisfaction with life are somewhat in an organized way. They may attract towards material values for the sake of maintenance of personal identities, strengthening interpersonal relationships, enhancement of personal experiences. These findings provide a blueprint to devise and pre-plan strategies and carefully monitor the exogenous agents who likely to contribute for materialistic values before it turns into pathological and destructive impulse for materialistic acquisitions among members of our society

The possible limitations of the present study included an overrepresentation of younger participants, future studies could include equal representation of participants from different age groups. The present investigation was a correlation; in future, the longitudinal nature of study could provide greater insight into the change in materialistic values over time in several age cohorts. Also, the study included participants from only from one city of Pakistan (i.e., Karachi), sample recruited from different cities of Pakistan enhance the Generalizability of findings all over the country.

Conclusion

The present findings provide useful insights about the positive linkages between materialism and life satisfaction among Pakistani nationals. The study pointed out the responsibility of media professionals and government to provide control for the increasing trend of materialism which found to be linked with life satisfaction of individuals. Also, present inquiry signify the role of mental health professionals and research scholars to educate about various personal and social factors that cause people to aspire for material pursuits; provide coaching to effectively deal and control the unhealthy consumption and compulsive materialism to promote and maintain the psychological well being of Pakistani nationals.

References

Anila, A.M., & Ismail, Z. (2005). Development of social support scale. *Pakistan Journal of Psychology*, 6(1); 26.

Baker, A. M., Moschis, G. P., Ong, F. S. & Pattanapanyasat, R. (2013). Materialism and life satisfaction: The role of stress and religiosity. *Journal of Consumers Affairs*, 47(3), 548-563.

Belk, R.W.(1984).Three scales to measure constructs related to materialism, reliability, validity and relationships to measures of happiness. *Advances in Consumer Research*, 11th ed. *Thomas Kinnear, Provo, UT: Association for Consumer Research*, 291 297.

Belk, R. W. (1985). Materialism: Trait aspects of living in a material world. *Journal of Consumer Research*, 12, 265-280.

Belk, R. W. (1988). Possessions and the extended self. *Journal of Consumer Research*, 15(2), 139-168.

Brouskeli, V., & Loumakou, M. (2014). Materialism, stress and health behaviors among future educators. *Journal of Education and Training Studies*, 2(2), 145-150.

Burroughs, J, E., & Aric, R.(2002). Materialism and well-being: A conflicting values perspective. *Journal of Consumer Research*, 29, 348-370.

Christopher, A. N., Marek, P. & Carroll, S. M. (2004). Materialism and attitudes toward money: An exploratory investigation. *Individual Differences Research*, 2(2), 109-117.

Churchhill, G. A. & Moschis, G. P. (1979). Television and interpersonal influences on adolescent consumer learning. *Journal of Consumer Research*, 6, 23- 34.

Csikszentmihaly ,M .(2005). Materialism and the evolution of consciousness. Kasser T, Kanner A.D. Editors. *Psychology and consumer culture*. Washington: American Psychological Association, 91-104.

Dawson, S., & Gary, B. (1991). If "We Are What We Have," What Are We When We Don't Have?. *Journal of Social Behavior and Personality*, 6 (6), 363-384.

Diener, E., Emmons, R. A., Larson, R. J., & Griffin, S. (1985). The satisfaction with life scale. *Journal of Personality Assessment*, 49, 71-75.

Diener, E., Oishi, S., & Lucas, R. E. (2003). Personality, culture, and subjective well-being: Emotional and cognitive evaluations of life. In S. T. Fiske, D. L. Schacter & C. Zahn-Waxler (Eds.), Personality, culture, and subjective well-being: Emotional and cognitive evaluations of life. *Annual Review of Psychology* (pp.403–425). Palo Alto, CA: Annual Reviews.

Ger, G. & Belk, R. W. (1996). Cross-cultural differences in materialism. *Journal of Economic Psychology*, 17, 55-77.

Golberg, M. E., Gorn, G. J., Peracchio, L. A. & Bamossy, G. (2003). Understanding materialism among youth. *Journal of Consumer Psychology*, 13(3), 278-288.

Hudders, L., & Mario, P. (2011). The silver lining of materialism: The Impact of luxury consumption on subjective well-being. *Journal of Happiness Studies*, 13(3), 391-404.

Inglehart, R. (2000). Globalization and postmodern values. *The Washington Quarterly*, 23(1), 215–228.

Kashdan ,T.B. & Breen ,W.L. (2007) Materialism and diminished well-being: Experiential avoidance as a mediating mechanism. *Journal of Social and Clinical Psychology*, 26, 521–539.

Kasser, T.& Ahuvia, A C.(2002). Materialism values and well-being in business students. *European Journal of Social Psychology*, 33(1), 137-146.

Kasser, T., Ryan, R. M., Zax, M. & Sameroff, A. (1995). The relations of maternal and social environments to late adolescents' materialistic and prosocial values. *Developmental Psychology*, 31, 907-914.

Kasser, T., & Ryan, R.M. (1996). Further examining the American dream: Differential correlates of intrinsic and extrinsic goal. *Personality and Social Psychology Bulletin*, 22, 280-287.

Kilbourne, William, Marko, G., & Janice, F. (2005). A cross-cultural examination of the relationship between materialism and individual values. *Journal of Economic Psychology*, 26(5),624-64.

Miller, M.G., & Rebecca L. T. (2009). Discretionary activity and happiness: The role of materialism. *Journal of Research in Personality*, 43 (4), 699-702.

Pavot, W., & Diener, E. (1993). Review of the satisfaction with life scale. *Psychological Assessment, 5*, 64- 172.

Pavot, W., & Diener, E. (2008). The satisfaction with life scale and the emerging construct of life satisfaction. *Journal of Positive Psychology, 3*, 137-152.

Polak, E. L.,& Michael E. M.(2006). Is gratitude an alternative to materialism? *Journal of Happiness Studies*, 7, 343-360.

Pollay, R. W. (1986). The distorted mirror: Reflections on the unintended consequences of advertising. *Journal of Marketing, 3*, 18-36.

Richins, M. L., & Dawson, S. (1992). A consumer values orientation for materialism and its measurement: scale development and validation. *Journal of Consumer Research, 19,* 303-316.

Richins, M. L. (2004). The material values scale: Measurement properties and development of a short form. *Journal of Consumer Research, 31,* 209-219.

Rindfleisch, A., Burroughs, J.E., & Wong, N. (2009). The safety of objects: Existential insecurity, and brand connection. *The Journal of Consumer Research, 36,* 1–16.

Roberts, J. A. (1998). Compulsive buying among college students: An investigation of its antecedents, consequences, and implications for public policy. *Journal of Consumer Affairs,* 32(2), 295-319.

Ryan, L., & Dziurawiec, S. (2001). Materialism and its relationship to life satisfaction. *Social Indicators Research,* 55, 185-197.

Ryan, R. & Deci, E. (2000). Self-determination theory and facilitation of intrinsic motivation, social development, and well-being. *American Psychologist,* 55, 68-78.

Sheldon, K. M. & Lawrence Krieger, S. (2014). Service job lawyers are happier than money job lawyers, despite their lower income. *The Journal of Positive Psychology,* 9(3), 219-2.

Sirgy, M.J. (1998). Materialism and the quality of life. *Social Indicators Research, 43(3),* 227-260.

Tatzel, M. (2003). The art of buying: Coming to terms with money and materialism. *Journal of Happiness Studies, 4(4),* 405-435.

Tuan, Y. (1980). The significance of the artifact. *Geographical Review,* 70(4), 462-472.

Wong, N., Shrum, L. J., Arif, F., Chugani, S., Gunz, A., Lowrey, T. M., Nairn, A., Pandelaere, M., Ross, S. M., Ruvio, A., Scott, K. & Sundie, J. (2011). Rethinking materialism: A process view and some transformative consumer research implications. *Journal of Research for Consumers,* 19, 1-4.